"I Guess I Do"

The Ultimate Marriage Survival Guide

Book Two: Best Practices for Marriage

By Ben Donley

Jock and Lola Publishing
The Coast in Beverly Hills, CA 90210
The Windmill Ranch in Snyder, TX 79550

Copyright © 2014

Printed in the United States of America

Dedicated to M.R.

Renewal…

6

Foreword by Michael Arnold, Psy.D., M.A.C.L.

Passion, conviction, candor, and definitely some Radiohead. That's what I think of when reflecting on my friend Ben. I have seen him stand up and speak about life, relationships, and one's personal journey in ways that leave his fingerprints all over the message. This is not because he is selfish or lobbying for attention. What leaves the indelible mark is his authenticity and unapologetic will to shoot it straight from his perspective. If you have heard him speak, read his books, or know him personally, it is easy to appreciate the vivid imagery he sees in the world, his honest struggles with the world's effect on its inhabitants, as well as his drive to be part of the solution.

My passion and time has been spent learning how to listen. I am a counselor. My goal is to come alongside others in a way that helps them learn how to both be and discover themselves in a way that is life giving. I see marriage as the ultimate test shedding light on this ever-changing identity process, both as individuals and as partners.

Sometimes as couples we do not like what we see, or perhaps, are thrown off when we realize reality is not even close to what we expected together. Do not give up, because there is hope. Ben uses his gifts to provide insight, wisdom, and practical tools you can use to either help set the foundation for your relationship or make some much-needed calibrations to a connection that has become distant and unclear. In the pages to come I am confident you can find yourself, your place, and your purpose in that thing we call marriage. Enjoy the ride and maybe a little Radiohead too.

Preface

I Guess I Do: The Ultimate Marriage Survival Guide – Best Practices in Marriage is the second book in a trilogy of self-help relationship books. This three book series aims to challenge every reader:

--To do some major pre-marital preparation by asking the Frequently UnAnswered Questions (FUAQs) before a wedding ceremony happens.

--To make use of the best relational practices so that you end up being a marriage winner rather than one of the ever-growing population of divorcees.

--To avoid the major and minor "marriage killers," which abound in most homes across this country and beyond.

**This relationship series is unlike anything you have ever read in that it tackles those topics most other relationship books fail to touch (and does so in fierce but fun ways). Prepare to laugh, to squirm, to discover, and to vastly improve on your side of the spousal equation.

Acknowledgements

Special thanks go out to all of the following humans who have helped with this marriage guide. First and foremost, all of the couples that have allowed me to learn from them as they prepared for, suffered from, and even enjoyed marriage while in my presence. Without you, I would only have statistics and research...

*****

--Marianne Randals, my close friend and business partner.

--HJ Swinford for formatting so "elegantly."

--Kevin Rhoads for being a superstar friend and designer.

--Connie Nugent for being a genius editor.

--My Book Ambassadors and Peer Influencers.

--Jock and Lola Publishing Group.

--My A-Team.

Who is this book written for?

--This book is written for those who have already gotten married and would prefer to have a really happy relationship rather than to have to survive a heart-breaking day-to-day grind. (80% of couples report having a miserable marriage relationship.)

--This book is written for those who have already been chewed up and spit out by marriage and are still trying to figure out why.

--This book is for those who want to be fully realistic and emotionally intelligent about the challenges inherent to marriage rather than living in the "Happily Ever After" dream world of how marriage is presented in both cultural myth and childhood imaginations.

--This book is for those who are willing to ask the important and necessary questions so they are prepared to be the best possible husbands and wives for as long as they shall live.

--This book is also for me so I can read it and remember to be a better relational human.

I am not Dr. Drew, so this might get weird, but so does marriage, and this book will help you do better than you would without it.

Welcome to Book Two!!!

Here's an intriguing question to begin: What if author Nicholas Sparks (*The Notebook*) started writing a screenplay about love, romance, and marriage and then halfway through, handed his manuscript over to two masters of horror, Wes Craven (*Nightmare on Elm Street*) and Stephen King (*The Shining*) so they could finish it up for an audience's viewing pleasure?

Can you imagine how that movie would begin and end? Can you imagine the shifts in tone, style, dialogue, character, plot, and climax as this film made its way from author to author to author? The difference would be striking and probably disturbing for the viewer and probably deeply confusing for those trying to craft a story about love descending into increasing horror.

Thankfully, this story won't be coming soon to a theatre near you, but it has seemingly been *green-lighted* by plenty of marriage partners in the 3-D worlds of the every day. The close-up movement from cute and sappy to confused and sad then finally to dangerous, frightening, and painful is becoming far too common inside your standard three-bedroom, two-bath houses across the country.

Can't we do something to make this odd "screenplay" uncommon? I think it's time we learn to rewrite for ourselves.

Marriage Case Study:

"Love and Horror"

John and Lorena Bobbitt

I am sure most of you have heard about this married couple. But just to quickly summarize for those who have not been subjected to the scoop, John and Lorena Bobbitt did not do too well after saying "I do." In their most famous incident, after a heavy night of drinking, John allegedly came home, raped his wife and then fell asleep. Lorena, who was angry about being taken advantage of, did not fall asleep. Instead, she went to the kitchen, found a carving knife, took it back to the master bedroom and proceeded to chop off half of her beloved husband's penis. (I pause and am thankful that there was no carrot shaver or cheese grater in sight.)

Lorena then took the half-penis of her *partner for life* and drove around in a state of confusion before rolling her window down and tossing John's half-penis out into a field. Wow. Then she called 911, reported her samurai skills, and turned herself into the police.

As John was being treated by a local hospital for whatever you want to call this assault (*over-circumcision* maybe), the cops sent out a search team who did an exhaustive treasure hunt and finally located the other half of John's vital organ, which they packed in ice and brought to the hospital. After about ten hours of surgery, John's penis was re-attached and from what I hear is doing fine to this day.

After this happened, John and Lorena Bobbitt *shockingly* divorced following six years of a marriage filled with emotional, physical, and mental abuse.

There is much more to this story, but what I am left wondering is: How does something like this happen between two people who fell in love, got engaged, exchanged rings, and said "I do?" How does a googly-eyed love fest move away from romance and connection to disdain and neglect followed by harsh responses, which then destroy the lives of the participants?

(Truth: It does not take a sharp knife on a private part to separate a man from a woman; sharp tongues have done just as much damage.)

While we do not imagine that your marital experience will at all resemble the Bobbitt experience, we still want to give you a little love-boost by offering some ideas, which will help your marriage be happily *unified* in every area – both public and *privates*. Seriously, no matter where you are in your marriage, even if you already have a weapon picked out for "separation" (or a divorce lawyer chosen), open your mind, read this book and try to humbly implement what we suggest. The advice within has helped so many people and can help you bring back that loving feeling.

Being Married

Okay. So you did it. You found someone who agreed to enter into the world of marital bliss with you and you both have rings to prove it. Prince Charmin' and Unsleeping Beauty standing side by side ready to share a bed and a life together forever.

Forever!!!

Forever…

Forever?

I wrote the following chapters to help you live out a satisfying life covenant even after the charm and the beauty wear off. The majority of married couples do not survive beyond the four-year mark, but I believe that if you use what follows, you cannot only beat the odds but you *can* live happily ever after.

Let's begin with an honesty exercise:

The Good, the Bad, and the Felonies

What do you know about yourself and how do you treat yourself as a result of this knowledge?

Before we move to the study of two people trying to become one, how about we start with just one key player – YOU.

How well do you know yourself?

Most people have no clue who they really are. Their identity is typically based on surface descriptions and expectations laid on them by teachers, parents, peers, and culture. Not much personal introspection is done at the deeper emotional levels and thus most people sort of just walk around behaving in a *what you see is what you get* shallowness. The intricacies of their design, the very nuances of their internal and external grand beauty, which makes each of them special, gets shrouded and hidden.

They act and react and respond and speak and emote and choose and even marry without much consideration of who they are. They have a name and a driver's license and a social security number and some credit cards, which allow them movement in this world of ours, but most lack a deep sense of self, which should be closely inspected.

Without a strong sense of personal identity, those who enter relationships requiring intimacy with a significant other often find themselves unable to show their deeper selves in vulnerable ways. And in a marriage, depth and vulnerability are expected and maybe even required.

Your spouse *will* be observing you and wondering why you do what you do and asking why you think the way you think and why you believe the way you believe. Will you know how to respond?

You should start asking the questions: Who am I apart from the description everyone else has laid on me all my life? Who is the "deeper me," and how can this true identity drive me to act in ways that will support and encourage a human I choose to love for life?

Now without further ado, let's exercise...

The Good, the Bad, and the Felonies:

Your Résumé and Anti-Résumé

The following exercise is designed to be a revelation for everyone who takes it seriously. Just follow the instructions and then I'll explain why it has major value for you.

On one side of a piece of paper write down "My Résumé" and then start a list underneath it with everything that makes you a good catch – think of it like you are coming up with a listing for a relational résumé – all the good, great, and grand things about you – nothing you would be ashamed of. Write down just the best stuff, which might get you *hired* by a species of the opposite sex.

(If you regularly save humans from drowning, visit nursing home castaways, and have body sweat that smells like tiramisu, these would be good things to put on that side of the paper.)

Throw all of your accomplishments, awards, characteristics, and masteries on there. This is the good version of you. The good person you would typically date with – *the special one you take to relational interviews* so a potential mate will not see your flaws and seek *greener humans.*

After you finish this, draw a vertical line down the middle of your paper and at the top of on the other side write the words, "My Anti-Résumé." Underneath this heading, write everything else about yourself - the bad, the ugly, the awful, and the gross. Put down stuff you want to hide away and let no one see. For instance, if you secretly eat your earwax or enjoy impersonating Charles Manson, make sure to include it on this list. Be as vulnerable as possible. Even include little stories that point to detailed accounts of your acting horrible to fellow humans, yard turtles or golden retrievers. Remember, this list reflects the "strange version of you" no one would date, hire, or hang out with if they knew about it. And this is the version of you who will come out later as a special wedding present to your spouse.

Jekyll might get most of the airtime, but Hyde won't stay hidden forever. Come on. Go ahead. Hold nothing back. Expose thy whole self to yourself.

Then pat yourself on the shoulder blades for the one *good* side of the list and cower in fear when you look at the other *bad* side. (If you are like me, you will probably need several sheets of paper to cover the bad stuff.)

Check out an example on the following pages. It might give you some ideas for your own résumé and anti-résumé.

My Résumé	My Anti-Résumé
--Tennis champion	--Nose picker
--Excellent dancer	--Line dancer
--Well-employed & salaried	--Toenail eater
--Has solid friendships	--Does not return phone calls
--Hilarious and clever	--OCD diagnosis
--Great counselor/listener	--Insecure and jealous
--Full head of hair	--Troubled with lice
--Romantic lover	--Snores like a chainsaw
--Loves Radiohead	--Piñata hoarder
--Saved a drowning dolphin	--Keeps penguin in freezer
--Drives a nice car	--Punches strangers in face
--Winner w/much potential	--The sorest loser on planet

My Résumé	My Anti-Résumé
--Adds value to all jobs	--Holds long-term grudges
--Active churchgoer	--Sleeps during sermons
--Loves *Mad Men*	--Acts like Don Draper
--Self-motivated go-getter	--Blames everyone
--Understands newest technology	--Plays PS3 5 hours per day
--Has sweet style	--Insecurity driven
--Travels extensively	--Thinks scrapbooking is #1
--Watches weight	--Tweets 40 times a day
--Great communicator	--Blogs about reality shows
--Known for wisdom	--Facebook over-poster
--Published author	--Wants to be like Poe
--Employs large vocabulary	--Mispronounces big words

<u>My Résumé</u>	<u>My Anti-Résumé</u>
--Good sense of direction	--Unreasonable expectations
--Punctual for all events	--"Seasonal" Vicodin addict
--Creative dater	--Super stubborn arguer
--Empowers those he/she dates	--Has evil motives & monocle
--Compliments people	--Keeps a secret "hit list"
--Pulled baby from alligator's mouth	--Shot Grandma w/pellet gun
--Bailed a buddy out of jail	--Farts during meals
--Donates to numerous charities	--Makes constant excuses
--Buys generous gifts for friends	--Erases other people's TiVo
--Got someone a much-needed job	--Lies on their résumé
--Nice singing voice	--Only sings "John Jacob Jingleheimer Schmidt"

What is the obvious?

The résumé says "I am a heroic person who is a great catch for any person or company. My behavior, attitude and history should get me loved, rewarded, and pleasantly eulogized at the time of my death."

The anti-résumé says "I am a villainous person who is a potential danger to anyone who enters my life bubble. My behavior, attitude, and history should get me professionally caned and/or tossed into the woods at my funeral."

More on this:

Why did I ask you to do this exercise?

The point of this exercise is to help you uncover your true and whole being using honesty and humility. It is suggested so you can come to grips with the fact that you are a beautiful, cool, interesting, foul, and messed-up human being, with a heart of gold *and* a gutter mind (or vice versa). It is to remind you that you are a professional shape-shifting chameleon who loves old people and kitty cats but who steals your neighbor's newspaper and secretly wants to remove the vocal cords from their yappy dog. A dark Sith lord and a Luke Skywalker rolled into one Jedi sushi roll.

It is meant to illustrate that you are both what you show and what you do not show. You are complicated and imperfect but reveal signs of goodness.

It is meant to "force" those who are typically too hard on themselves to admit some positives about their *being* so they don't walk around in insecure humiliation speaking out negative self-talk with every sentence. "Stop beating the hell out of yourself, friend!!! You are not as bad as you think."

It is also meant to *force* overly-optimistic narcissists to recognize the ugly and imperfect spots about themselves so they don't strut around in constant cocky self-congratulations refusing to see they are capable of being the problem. Stop patting yourself on the back and thinking you can do no wrong. You may be such a master of hiding your crap that you have fooled even yourself thus far, but you too have a massive anti-résumé, which needs to be accounted for and definitely tamed.

And if you are somewhere in the middle of our humiliated group and overly-confident crowd, this exercise was meant to keep you from leaning too hard one way or the other in certain situations.

Also, here is the thing: You do not need to be too proud of one side or too ashamed of the other. You are a balance of weird, gross, lovely, and special. And if some people knew the whole of what sort of person you are, if they knew both sides of the page, they would run for the hills as they screamed to passersby the cruel truth about your revealed ugliness.

No matter. Let's wreck the façades anyway. Accept the balance of our résumé and anti-résumé. And most important, begin to love ourselves enough that we don't live to cover up the bad or exist to let everyone know how badly we suck.

Be secure in knowing that everyone is both cool and messed up and then start giving love to yourself.

This self-love/self-security will make you more patient in your search for a mate. Loved people are less likely to rush into a relationship because they already have most of what they need.

Getting this self-acceptance out of the way will keep you from choosing someone out of neediness (who can fill in your gaping holes) or from subjecting yourself to some psycho bad boy/girl so that you can punish yourself for being such a "piece of crap" undeserving of anything resembling love.

When you can accept and love yourself at your worst the same as how you accept and love yourself at your best, not based on résumé or anti-résumé, you can live free.

And when you live free, you can attract people who will love you as you deserve - fully and unconditionally.

When people come to me for pre-marital or early marital counseling, I sometimes suggest that they do this exercise together so that they can go ahead and get everything out on the table. It saves a ton of energy not having to play hide and seek. It keeps you from the pressures of having to live up to a résumé. It also keeps the other person from being shocked when he/she finds a dead cow in the trunk of your automobile. (They already knew you were "udderly" crazy anyway before they popped open the back of your Lincoln Town Car.)

Truth is: This exercise is important to do for you whether you *share* the toughest stuff or not. You get to decide how much you tell. Just realize that overt vulnerability can be a good thing and a relational game changer.

Why?

When you can be vulnerable, you welcome the ones around you to be the same, and you help to make real relationships possible. The stupid games people play with one another in the dating and early marriage life are pretty much destroyed with a few shared lists. And when freedom and security are the foundation of your identities, there is never a need for a double life, nor is there the deadly insecurity, which makes people do the stupidest things within dating and marriage relationships.

I could go on an on about this issue for chapters, but let's just assume most of us have insecurities, which currently drive much of our decision-making within relationships, leading to bad ends. It does not have to be this way.

If you begin to let go of any self-hate, stop arguing with either side of the previous lists, accept yourself and let others know up front that regardless of the résumé and the anti-résumé, you are going to make relational decisions based on the security founded on the balanced love of a screwed-up self (and you will end up just fine).

That being said: I am not trying to give license to those of you who might want to use this exercise to bolster your "This is just who I am" excuse for not changing the crazy parts of your anti-résumé. I am a major proponent of discovering and sharing all parts of your self with your significant other and cutting yourself some slack, killing insecurity dead, and finding a balanced humility. But even more so, I will insist to everyone that just because you can now "accept" what you have admitted to be "you," you must also enter into a process of shutting down the most relationally annoying and potentially destructive parts of your anti-résumé.

Being an occasional oddity is normal.

Being a habitual freak is not.

You have to stop repeatedly doing *unacceptable* things that burn bridges, damage others, cause friction, and lead to greater separations.

Some questions to consider:

What parts of the résumé do you try to emphasize so that you can look good to the world and to the opposite sex?

What parts of your anti-resume make you feel unworthy and disgusted with yourself?

What do you need to do to live as the full human – the good, bad, and the ugly – that you are?

When do you think you are you going to be able to be fully vulnerable within yourself and then accept both sides of the page as true but irrelevant to your deeper identity?

Okay. Enough exercising. (We don't want to pull any reputation hamstrings or overdo your core training.)

Let's go ahead and get all of you bi-behavioral spouses a few useful *best practices*, which will hopefully help you overcome the innate relational stupidity that exists in every man and woman who walks on the earth.

Now that you have admitted you are at least a partial moron in the initial exercise, you should be more than prepared to accept these humble offerings, which come from years of observation, experience, growth, and pain.

Best Practice #1:

Keep winning them

So much effort goes into winning someone's heart.

"When we find 'the one', we tend to throw everything we can at getting them to fall in love with us." They take over our minds and our emotions. We become convinced that we cannot live without them and so we make it our absolute priority to woo them. This wooing requires all of our best ideas, best hygiene, best clothes and best conversations. We listen harder to everything they have to say. We buy them the things they like. We write them notes. We pen them poetry. We create mix CDs and Spotify Playlists for them. We tell them the most intimate details from our histories. We get vulnerable. We stop belching and "re-arranging" in public. We dress nice. We smell nice. We speak every *love language* on the planet. We ignore their faults and even consider their idiosyncrasies "cute." We lose sleep for them. We choose them over our friends and our fun and our work. We pray more than ever that God will close the deal for us.

Both men and women become focused conquerors who must "take the *land* or die trying." Romantic Rubicons and Common Sense be damned!!!

And if all works out and the other person responds favorably to our efforts, we make the culturally appropriate advances, which can lead to the ultimate goal - a marriage ceremony.

Ah yes, taking the slow walk in society's best fashion during a sacred hour surrounded by closest friends and family; staring into each other's eyes and speaking out those words of absolute victory, "I do." And with that, we take a deep breath and realize, "I did it." This other person is now *ours*. We have crossed the Finish Line and can now go to the Honeymoon Trophy presentation.

Yes!!!

High fives and aluminum cans tied to the back of our vehicle as we drive away into a certain "Happily Ever After" where fun and joy and happiness await us.

But somehow, more than one out of every two of these marriages ends in divorce. And only about 15% of those 40% who make it without a complete breakdown, actually experience the hoped-for, long-term marital bliss.

The big question is why…

Why do these love affairs fall apart? Why do people who believed so much in each other and who worked so hard to make a deep connection stop loving each other?

I cannot speak to everyone's specific situation. But I think I have figured out some general themes, which may shed some light on the majority of failing marriages.

Problem I: The Mindset Changes

When we are dating and pursuing, we usually have the mindset of a Winner (please differentiate here between our version and Charlie Sheen's version of *winning*). We see someone whom we want to be with and we do all we can to win his/her heart. But when we step out of that ceremony, hand in hand with our spouse, we have achieved the big victory. In a way, we think we have already won and no longer feel the need to be in winner mode. And thus we tend to change our mindset from Winner to Owner. "I have you and you have me." And once this shift happens in our heads, a terrible shift happens in our actions.

What occurs?

As Owners, we tend to relax. We stop doing what we did when we were in Winner mode. We quit doing what we did to win that person's heart. We function like, "This person is mine now. I cannot lose them." And then the worst thing of all happens: We begin to take our spouses for granted.

And when we take our spouses for granted, we actually do start to lose them. We move from Heart-Winners to Heart-Losers. It happens all the time.

Problem II: Acting like Losers

What does "losing" look like?

--Moving from Multi-lingual to Mute – When we were winning, we spoke every love language in the book. We gave gifts. We offered our most quality time. We served them. We spoke uplifting and encouraging words. We comforted and even made them feel cared for with our physical touch. But now that we no longer have that *healthy pressure* to do so, we pull back. We go mute. We slow down on the gifts, take back our time, groan at having to serve, use our words for "house business," and we slowdown/stop the affectionate touching.

--The Priority List Shifts – When we were winning, our significant other was placed at the very top of our list and everything else was ordered below them. This person got all of our attention because they were our most important pursuit. But after we successfully conquered them, our "significant other" got much less significant as they are taken out of the front seat and off of the front burner. They get moved down.

Moved down to where?

Moved back down below *everything* that was ranked high on the "life list" before that person entered into the picture. *Everything* - including endless career ladders, childhood friendships, unfulfilled dreams, unseen movies, unseen television series, unfinished video games, unPinned recipes, shopping lists, other people, cool events, unvisited vacation spots, and other *un-owned* opportunities. These take precedence. Most of the time it is a subconscious re-prioritizing, because nobody really writes "tossing the love of my life to the back burner," on a literal to-do list. Still, the reality happens and can be seen in the behavior of one or both marriage participants.

--The Anti-Love happens – Somehow when we are dating, we are able to accomplish the best version of "love" more than ever. As Winners, we tend to be patient, kind, trusting, humble, truthful, forgiving, and selfless. But as Owners, we not only stop loving, we also begin to distribute what I call "the Anti-Love." We treat our spouses with selfishness, impatience, unkindness, jealousy, competitiveness, a lack of forgiveness, and pride.

--We stop trying to be attractive – When we were trying to woo our spouses, we did all we could to put on our best faces. But as Owners, we put our best faces away and often stop trying to be attractive at all. We think that once we get married it is unnecessary to attract our mates. We act as if their life commitments to us give us license to *let ourselves go.*

Our Ugly Reality becomes 3-D. Our morning breath goes unchecked. The bathroom door is left open during what used to be private stench sessions. Toilets go unwiped. Matches go unlit. Body odor is allowed to reign. Pounds are added by the baker's dozen, lips are left chapped, and we let ourselves go on one-way trips to unattractiveness. We get gross, act impolitely, and assume that our partners' sensory organs are dead.

--Baggage Claim Time – When we are winning our partners' hearts, we do not usually parade around our unstable emotional, mental, and spiritual baggage. In Winner mode, we understand that carrying this sort of crazy life baggage around is scary to potential suitors. If we want people to take lifetime trips with us, we know that we had better not show up to the "Marriage

40

Airport" with more than a small suitcase and a carry-on. Yes, we may reveal some of our smaller issues, but nothing that will alarm the ones we love.

But, when we do *land* our partners and the marriage happens, most of us believe it will be okay if we go ahead, grab all of our pseudo-psycho luggage off of the airport carousel (that we so carefully checked before take-off), and then ask our partners to help us carry it.

This can be a shocking event when the Owner of said baggage gets past the Honeymoon then rents three Smart Carts and loads on huge trunks packed tight with past rejections, insecurities, anger, bitterness, family addiction patterns, and unstitched wounds. These get rolled to the car and then carried into the marriage.

Eyes get wide when this sort of unpacking begins.

"Can all that crap really be yours, sweetheart?" Sweetheart nods her head, but not sweetly.

--Role changes – When we are actively winning people's hearts, we smartly take on the role of lover and ally. These are the parts we play. These roles define the script we speak. They guide the actions we take. But when we become Owners, we often exchange our positive roles for negative ones. Instead of lifting our partners up, we become critics who give thumbs down to most of their moves. Instead of applauding their goodness, we become nags who demand quick changes. Instead of acting as their equal partners in the business of marriage, we take on the role of boss and act as if they owe us quality work.

Surprise: Nobody enjoys a micromanaging critic trying to mold him/her into a desired shape. This will not work for long.

Now, I am not saying that everyone reading this book has gone from being a Heart Winner to becoming a full-scale Heart

Loser. But almost without exception, marriage participants display some of the behavioral shifts described above. If you are honest in your personal evaluation, you will probably notice that you too have become somewhat less of a Winner and more of a Spouse Loser. And if this is true, and you have intentionally or unintentionally gone in this direction with your mindset and your actions, I have something very important to write to you here:

You may "have" your partner legally, but by owning them you are losing them daily, and you deserve to lose them. The love you once earned and the heart you once won is now being given back.

One of the main causes of divorce and cheating is that one or both people within the marriage stop doing what they did before they got married.

It is a simple equation really: Winners who become Owners usually become Losers. This is not to say that you will necessarily lose your marriage and end up alone, but I can pretty much guarantee that the love your partner had for you before the "I do" will wane. And since marriage is supposed to be a relationship filled with love, a marriage that begins leaking love is going to feel very flat very soon.

Are you rolling around on a flat marriage?

No matter who you are, I would recommend taking a close look at the marriage relationship you are in. Ask honest questions of yourself. Also, invite your partner to weigh in. Find out from him/her if you are acting more like a Winner or an Owner. If you discover symptoms of this shift, keep reading to check out how to end the losing streak.

Best Practice #2:

Stop your Losing Streaks

How To End a *Losing Streak* in Marriage

Hey, dummy. You are not alone in your spousal idiocy. I've worked with hundreds of bad Owners and relational Losers during my work days. And, I'll admit that I've been a very bad Owner and a relational Loser during the many years of my marriage. From experience, I can assure you that if you act like this for sustained periods/eras/epochs of time you can count a closedown of marital bliss.

Losing streaks are deadly. They must be noted and stopped before they lead to relational flat lines.

The good news is that just because you are currently an Owner/Loser combination does not mean you have to stay that way. You don't have to just helplessly watch as your marriage ebbs away. You can actually do some things about your situation to put an end to your losing streaks. Are you interested in stopping your slump and breaking the streak? Do you want to become the heart champion you once were?

If so, I suggest reading the rest of this book and applying what I advise. I know that you can apply the following and thrive. I'll bet you can start your winning ways again soon.

43

How To End a *Losing Streak* in Marriage

Solution A.

Admit It: "I am not winning my wife/husband. I am actually acting in such a way that I am losing him/her. I need to get back into a Winner mode or somebody else is going to win them."

Every married person needs to keep in mind that there are plenty of single (plus a lot of unhappily married) people out there who are on the prowl for someone to love. This means that there are plenty of individuals on the planet who are in high-gear Winner mode. These people are at the top of their Winner games. They are doing all they can to *ATTRACT*. And if you happen to be living like an Owner, your spouse might start making the comparison. *Person A* is looking good, smelling good, and treating me with affection, while my spouse is looking rough, smelling like feet, and treating me like furniture.

Add this to the reality that not everyone out there is pulling for the continuation of your marriage. In other words, there are people who might want you to experience divorce so they can take hold of what you are losing. Times have changed. A large section of the population is not worried about upholding a moral code and/or some social contracts. They do not respect the ring. These opportunists just see a disappointed and tied down prize to take home with them. They want what you obviously do not. *So, if you are not treating your spouse as special, someone out there may be happy to do your job.*

How To End a *Losing Streak* in Marriage

Solution B.

Do what you did before you said, "I do"

Sit down with a pen and a piece of paper and answer the following questions:

How did I act when trying to get my partner to choose me?

Am I still acting this way?

What things did I do?

Am I still doing these things?

What specifically will I do to get back on the winning track?

Once you create a solid list, begin to do what you once did.

And once you start re-doing these things, keep them going until you die. Stop being lazy. Be a winner of a partner. Show everyone that you still adore the person you are married to.

Truth: Most people do not actually take out a piece of paper and a pen and write out answers to these questions. *But we should do it.* The effort means something. It tells our brains that we are taking this "daily winning" seriously. It shows we are not just keeping it in mind, but we are inking it as an outside reminder to be the best spouse we can be. It gives us something to look at so that we can gauge our current movements.

How To End a *Losing Streak* in Marriage

Solution C.

Grow Up

In my life I do not recall ever being told that I made the official move from boy to man. There was no ceremony or Mitzvah and there were no painful or purifying rites of passage – no one yelling in my ears or tattooing my skin that might have let me know that I was no longer a boy but a man. So, after I got married, I kept acting like the boy who needed his wife to take over mommy duties. It was only about five years ago that I realized I was being a boy instead of a man. It was time for me to stop playing the part of grabby toddler who justified every deed or non-deed with a tiresome excuse.

My suggestion to you would be to take a close look at your life – your words, your efforts, your responses/reactions, your work, etc. – and evaluate whether or not you are acting like a kid or an adult. Marriage is not a fun-time sandbox where tattle-tell blaming, excuse-making, rule-breaking, threatening, bullying, and name-calling works for very long. Marriage is more like an Exodus where both parts of the partnership are serious about journeying through to a better location.

So, we must grow up!!!

Quit acting like a spoiled little boy or girl!!!

Throw away your adult pacifiers, stop manipulating to get your way and do not throw tantrums every time life is not perfect. Your spouse is not your mama or your daddy. He/she did not get into this marriage to raise you, support you, buy you toys, cook your dinner, clean up your room, fix your hair, rock you to sleep, spank you and burp you. Your spouse did not sign up to take over where your parents left off or sign up to improve on where your parents failed.

Your husband or wife signed up to have a mature relationship with another mature adult.

So stop looking for a spouse who will change your diapers when you take a big life crap in your pull-up Pampers. Get some potty-training from an older mentor who has grown up and can show you how to make mistakes like a grown-up. In other words, learn how to act your age.

And, stop looking for a spouse who will pity you as you keep toddling around in your whiny "who am I?" twenties and thirties. Get a counselor, pastor, or life coach to help you move past your unwillingness to walk through your confusions and fears. *Blame* is for the very young but it gets old super fast.

And stop looking for a spouse who will coddle you and give you everything you want when you want it. Just cause your parents never told you "No" for fear that you might pout, scream, or run away does not mean you don't need to hear it a lot. Spoiled brat spouses make a lot of people want to pull out the proverbial paddle and smack them in the head.

Stop looking for a spouse who will tickle your little chinny-chin chin and coo over you and your accomplishments. You are not always cute. Sometimes you are annoying as hell. You are not always that great. Sometimes you are a total failure. Figure out how to live with those facts and without the constant applause!

Stop looking for a spouse who will allow your parents to keep parenting you after marriage.

And finally, stop being a spouse that enables this sort of childish behavior. You are just as bad if you don't insist on a process of increasing maturity first in yourself and then in your spouse.

Truth: All of us have areas of arrested development, but we don't have to let them imprison us. Make growing up a major goal as you consider the following:

What is maturity?

In what areas have I not grown up?

How can I become an adult spouse?

What sort of people do I need to add to my life so that I can have the right kind of modeling?

How To End a *Losing Streak* in Marriage

Solution D.

Ally

When you wake up in the morning next to your spouse, make the decision to become their chief ally and their biggest help. Realize that you are a part of a two-person team. You are not in competition with this person. You are in an alliance, which means you stand together against anyone and anything that threatens to keep either or both of you from living out an abundant life.

You do not look after just yourself. You also look after your person.

Find out what your spouse's life goals are and use your words and your actions to help him/her achieve them. Sometimes this will require you sacrificing what you want so that they can climb closer to what they are meant to be.

Do your partner favors.

Think of ways that you can create opportunities for them.

Forgive them if they let you down.

When you are in public together, speak highly of them and don't be critical or call them on *their stuff* around others. If you need to address something, do the diplomatic thing and lovingly talk about it with them at home.

Applaud their successes as you feed them helpful truths.

Remind them that they are lovable and valuable.

Ask them how you can do more to lift them up.

If you do these things, your spouse will know they are loved. They will realize that they do not walk this life alone. They will look at you and see you as an invaluable part of their life. They will be thankful and most likely reciprocate with similar actions. Your marriage will flourish if you commit yourself to such things.

Why show off the flaws of the one you love the most when you are meant to be the one they can count on to promote their best side?

Why not act as a constant encourager? Sure, you know their weaknesses better than anyone and you also probably know that their weaknesses easily outnumber their strengths. You have seen them fail up close and often and you have stories to tell – stories to bring the house down at your partner's expense. But why do it? It leaves them alone in their failures and erodes their confidence in you even if they laugh at the story and brush it off as if it did not hurt.

I am always amazed at couples that seem to be more enemies than friends – more competitive than cooperative. Couples who hold hands but who do not hold their spouses up as someone to admire. Couples who have made vows but who look at one another with disdain and speak of one another with disgust. Couples reminding the one supposedly closest to their hearts that they are foolish and embarrassing and capable of the most stupid things – bringing out those horrible anecdotes and staying quiet about the amazing pieces. Not being allies or lovers or friends at all, but mean burdens crying out to anyone with ears that they made a mistake. No grace exchanged, just harsh judgmental recollections of what has already been done wrong, which point to what will probably be again.

Recipe for disaster.

Make a decision with your spouse to shift in this area. Begin to only think of your spouse in noble and excellent ways. Think of all the ways they are awesome to you. Then let those thoughts become the public words you use to showcase them as your ally in this world.

You need one and they need one. Two against the world doubles your odds at victory.

How To End a *Losing Streak* in Marriage

Solution E.

Keep a Record of Rights

Husbands and wives keep vaults of the wrongs, the failures and the mistakes of their *better halfs*, carefully filing away insults, exclusions, failures, and pain. Then, when the time is right, usually as a fight escalates, both partners go to war with this old ammunition – flinging old truths and yet to be forgiven or forgotten wrongs into the others' faces. Basically being a personalized Accuser used to break apart the one they love in the most personal ways.

I am not sure if it is the idealization of a spouse which makes us do this or just the sense we have a right to kick the crap out of our best friend because we think they will let it go in time. Whatever drives this sort of behavior is unacceptable. In fact, I want to recommend that a list be made of all of these old wrongs so that each individual can set fire to their files giving forgiveness and forgetfulness a chance to rule the rest of marriage.

As well, I am calling on all spouses to use their now-emptied vaults to store up every good or right thing their spouse does or says.

Why don't we keep a record of rights?

Why are we not ready with the best words to say about our partners' best attempts so they can be lifted up rather than be torn down?

If we do not have these sorts of responses and reactions ready, then who will?

As it turns out in most cases, our spouses have plenty of self-hate in storage. They have their own negative audio files (junk about themselves) playing internally on constant repeat loops. As their best friend and ally, you can be the voice of kindness and positive focus that can snap apart the CD of accusations that their soul enemy has mixed-up for them.

A Brief Confession from a friend of mine whom I've counseled for a few years now:

"My wife leaves her brushed out hair in the tub, speeds without a seatbelt (and gets tickets), projects her work frustration on me, laughs at me when I spill scalding hot coffee on my hands, and presents our unknown future as a completely negative scenario we are sure not to survive. She also ignores me sometimes and gets angry when I don't bring home all the receipts so she can accurately do the budget. There are other things I could mention because I have them stored up in a safe box called "The Argument File," which is easily accessed when I need to defend any of my shortcomings (like losing at online poker, snoring, being overly friendly with strangers, and acting like a prideful teenager when losing at Words with Friends). It is a beautiful way to fight. If she comes at me with one of my wrongs then I simply pull out one of her wrongs, which is just a bit bigger than the one she just mentioned about me. Then she will pull out a bigger one than that one and then I will pull out a bigger one than that and soon both of us are standing there yelling about everything from these huge file cabinets of wrong that each of us do and have done. (I even have imaginary files ready.) Volleys upon volleys of verbal disrespect fired into the softest and most vulnerable areas and neither of us signing a treaty of "Sorry" till later on in the evening.

We still do this sometimes – especially when we are tired or sick – but it happens less often.

53

Why?

Not because the wrongs have stopped. In fact, the wrongs keep going on and new ones are added daily. I guess it occurs less because we have decided to intentionally close the books on the wrongs and rewrite a new file. Sure, we have a regular marriage meeting where we talk calmly about how each of us can increase the happiness of the other by becoming less annoying, but this happens over a nice meal and a glass of wine and in a spirit of mutual desire to improve for the other's sake. We also have determined to keep a record of rights handy so that we can *talk loudly* at each other about the cool things we see in one another.

My wife is super talented, one of the most generous people on the planet, a servant to all, a helper, and a brilliant mind, among a million other great things. The key for me is to choose words that reflect those positive records and allow them to trump the petty negative thoughts, which my arrogance and insecurity want me to use as a hatchet on my wife's esteem."

Thanks to my friend for his honest confessions.

Like him, we must all remember to lift our spouse up not take them down. We all need to be reminded of our own good. Do not keep a record of your spouse's wrongs. Keep track of their rights.

How To End a *Losing Streak* in Marriage

Solution F.

Re-Date

This is simple: When you Stop Scheduling Fun, You Start Dying.

Just because you don't have the hard-charging romance-driven *dopamine date rushes* you used to have, it does not mean you retire from plotting personalized, intentional fun-filled field trips for one another. (Unless you want to just be rent-sharing roommates who drive each other crazy trying to own the remote control.)

My re-dating recommendations are to step outside the norm, look up the surprisingly weird holidays/calendar celebrations (like *National Donut Day, International Jean-Claude Van Damme Movie Week* and *Interplanetary Sleep Naked in Saran Wrap Month*), choose one per month and then plan creative fun using the calendar suggestions as your underlying theme.

Anyone can pull off a sweet Valentine's Day with chocolate hearts, red roses, Olive Garden and double spouse lingerie time on the futon while watching *Casablanca*. It's time for couples to kick it up a notch and start taking partner pole dancing classes during *Find a Daring New Hobby Week*. Date boldly. Date intentionally. Date funny. Pre-meditate cool times with one another. This will keep your marriage as fresh as Febreze and hopefully make you both laugh enough in the undertakings that any future tears are trumped by the hilarity of past outings. If you are bad at coming up with ideas for this, there are plenty of great ideas out there in bookstores and on the Internet, which will ensure your significant other's happiness. Steal some of those and put them into practice.

How To End a *Losing Streak* in Marriage

Solution G.

Re-Visioning

Someone once said, "If you stare at a great work of art for years, it will become for you like a piece of junk not worthy to be hung on a special wall under special lighting, but instead to be passed by in favor of lesser versions."

I agree with that statement not only as it concerns gallery paintings and sculptures but also with how it applies to husbands and wives. I cannot even count how many couples I have dealt with in counseling who describe their very attractive other halves as *replaceable and regular paint by number pieces* after having seen them day in and day out for a few years. Instead of viewing them as walking, talking skin-canvas *Monsieur and Madame X* who deserve to be admired and hung up in their own personal Love-Louvre, amazing husbands and gorgeous wives get categorized as common caveman drawings or worse, *Whistler's Mother* and/or *American Gothic*.

If you are one of these people who has allowed your vision to be altered by time, I am going to suggest that you go beyond seeing your significant other as passing scenery and force yourself to view them anew from now on. Move beyond the general form and look for the details of their inner and outer beauty. Once I personally started doing this, I noticed things about my wife I had never seen before; the nuances of her freckle constellations and the subtle changes in her daily style. I now explore her with my eyes so that I know her better than anyone who has ever laid eyes on her. The little things make me thankful. When I pay attention to who

57

she is, I also begin to notice her emotional state by observing her body language, which has helps me to respond in the right ways to difficult days and various mood shifts.

So, it is not just about physical beauty, which *will* fade, but the current design, which points to the reality of who she is and who she will be as a whole person for all her days.

Once you try this approach, you will find yourself speaking good words to your chosen one and good words never hurt. Especially when you say something original about the depths of their fantastic paint strokes. You will not just be making "You look hot!" statements that could be uttered by any construction worker or Victoria Secret retail workers. You will utter deep compliments, which reflect that you are paying attention to parts of them – both surface and beneath – traits that they might not have considered. They will be uplifting words based on studied observation.

Too many times as *spouse-owners* we forget the amazing creations we have been given to borrow for a time. We take their canvas and use them as coasters for our Big Gulps as we watch other "fascinating people" on the television. No more coasting…

Summary: Okay, that is my own version of Lasik surgery for marriage. Now, you go get your corneas redone so you can have a re-visioning.

How To End a *Losing Streak* in Marriage

Solution H.

Re-Speak

Simple: Be fluent in the *Five Love Languages* as presented in the book of the same name by Dr. Gary Chapman. (For those of you unfamiliar with the five love languages, they are: Quality Time, Words of Affirmation, Acts of Service, Physical Touch, and Gift Giving.) I have read this excellent book several times and I regard it as a practical and helpful way to get couples to think differently about putting love into practice in ways which will deeply touch their spouse; to make them feel cherished in ways our partners can really experience it.

As a Winning spouse, one must make themselves intimately aware of their partner's primary and secondary love languages and then act in ways that support those languages.

*I counseled one guy we will simply call *Dumb Husband* (D.H.), whose wife was an *acts of service* and *quality time* girl, which meant that if he wanted to show his wife love that would both penetrate and stick, he needed to figure out what specific things he could do to make sure both of her languages got spoken. His woman was a clean freak and so I told D.H. he had to become a stud with a broom, a Swiffer, a sponge, some Pledge wipes, and a Hoover vacuum. I also advised him that he needed to pull himself away from TV sports and iPhone diversions so he could sit one-on-one with her, paying full attention to her words and affirming her as she tried to get to the bottom of different parts of her life. And over the first few years he made sure to become a listener who asked

59

informed questions without taking a cell call or responding to a text while she expressed herself. By his own report, D.H. also became a fairly good duster, underwear folder, Bounce changer, and toilet shiner. His wife noticed and his marriage went from a four to a nine.

But after a while, Ol' Dumb Husband got cocky. And he got lazy. And he found himself saying "No hablo love" a lot more. He had become Shakespearean in his relational oratory but as years passed, he found himself living off of the memories of what a great lover he used to be. And as expected, the nine dropped back down to a four. From being a fully fluent five-language wordsmith, he went mute in three of them and even went into *mumbler mode* with his wife's expressed love languages.

Dumb husband did the below:

Acts of Disservice - Dirty dishes stayed in the sink. Clean dishes stayed in the dishwasher. Bounce sheets get re-used for several cycles in a dryer with thick carpets of black lint creeping out of the lint screen. Plastic bottles and aluminum cans get tossed on the floorboard of the Toyota.

Under-Quality Time: - Sportscenter and NFL games remained on high volume when she told him about her day and he even played Star Wars Angry Birds while she detailed important stuff about her family and her future.

Why?

This guy started blaming his spouse for what he thought was something legitimate: her brazen refusal (read: "accidental") to "speak" to him in *his love languages*. How dare she expect him to take care of her love needs while she neglected his love needs. Unbelievable, right? Unacceptable, right? D.H. thought so.

So, he ignored me from then on and passive-aggressively pressed back into his leather couch waiting for some tit-for-tat to motivate him. "You love me the way I need, and I'll love you the way you want."

Don't be like this *Dumb Husband*. Hear me out where he would not and follow the advice below:

a. Don't be the Owner who thinks they are Owed!!!

b. No Tits-for-Tats!!!

c. Don't get into the very common tendency to punish your spouse by giving them the love silent treatment when they are frustrating you. To pull back from expressions of love because your spouse is not pulling their weight for a time will only lead to distance between you. And as distance happens, it becomes harder and harder to hear one another communicating.

d. Do get back to doing the maximum for your spouse. There are parts of their hearts that will light up when you give them meaningful compliments (words of affirmation) within an area of insecurity; when you gift them with something that they mentioned wanting six months ago (pay attention to everything they say and store it for the right moment); when you touch them in a way that may or may not lead to a *sexy-time* experience, but still shows that you notice them and are connected to them; when you plan out concentrated, close quarter conversations about life and when you serve them in a way that is meaningful.

Summary: The point I am making with all of this is that love languages can be spoken like a tourist struggling to find a bathroom in a foreign country using broken syllables from a phrasebook. Or, these love languages can be spoken like a fluent native who can express deep love from every angle. Why not take your bad language out of the baño and make it muy bonito?

How To End a *Losing Streak* in Marriage

Solution I.

Re-Branding (An Author's Confession)

In the "what I used to do" times, I put my relationship with my girlfriend, who became my wife, in the number one spot (and this could easily be seen in the amount of energy and time I put into growing and nurturing our relationship). But as time went on, I purposefully let her slip down below my job, my dreams, my writing, and my fun. And just as you would expect for "low-priority" things, she got much less attention. In fact, I saw her as more of a barrier that stood in the way of my chasing down the things I had yet to attain. She went from being a fun person to whom I wanted to give everything, to being a frustrating nagger with a to-do list at least a mile too long.

The interesting part is this: Only my mind had changed about my wife. Truth is, my woman had not changed a bit. She was not really a nagger with a bothersome to-do list. She was actually the same cool human I married. But I allowed my opinion about her to shift because I needed a good reason to justify my selfish pursuits. I basically branded her as an "enemy of my state of affairs" because it is easier to do what you want whenever you want when your closest relationship is officially listed as a *ball and chain* or *B&Cs*. *B&Cs* are easy to brush off, ignore, and treat badly. You can put them in their place and get away with it. Everyone understands and accepts the new branding because it conveniently allows for the best of both worlds – a working marriage and the ability to act like a foolish person who is trying with all their might to reach self-actualization.

So, we actually achieve marriage by setting aside our selfish priorities but then internally demonize our spouses mentally and sometimes publicly so we can then reclaim our trivial pursuits.

In light of that personal realization, I am asking all of you readers to be honest on this one. Have you branded your lover as a *Ball and Chain* or as an incessant whiner because he/she is a barrier to your individual desires?

If so, try re-branding. This person you are vilifying so you can justify your selfishness is actually your *BEST HALF*, who deserves to be raised back up to the top of your human priority list. Stop trying to actualize only your self and start trying to help your partner find their God-given space in the sun.

How To End a *Losing Streak* in Marriage

Solution J.

Re-Trying Harder

You don't think it's a bad thing to be attractive for your spouse post-marriage do you? Did a marriage therapist from the Kevorkian school of Counselors advise you to pull back on the reins of attraction after year one to see if your partner really meant their altar vows?

Many spouses do not seem to be trying very hard at maximizing their attraction potential.

Ask yourself the following:

Are you trying to be as attractive now as you once tried to be in the pre-marriage days? Are you trying to look as good for your spouse as you once did, or has there been some fallback?

It's okay if there has been some fallback. A few pounds here and there, extra wrinkles, and some tired bags under the eyes are to be expected. This is not a call to be a ten on the ten scale for your whole life. But I think it might be a good idea to keep the below info at the front of your mind.

Here is what I suggest: Attempt Attraction.

Being attractive is good. And, it does not have to cost you a lot of money or a lot of effort to maximize what you have been given.

Get some stylish clothes (TJ Maxx carries name brands for both sexes), a cool hairstyle (choose the hippest looking person at Fantastic Sam's), some toned body parts (forget Cross-Fit for now – just do several push-ups, sit-ups, and take the stairs wherever you are), stand in the backyard sun for 15 minutes every once in a while in your undergarments to tan your vampire paleness, and eat a healthy diet at around 2,000 calories per day (not three times per day).

Consider this: Gaining five pounds per year, which would actually be on the *miracle* side of most American realities, will mean you will be one hundred pounds heavier on your twentieth anniversary. Scale that for yourself and determine if an extra hundred would make you happy, much less make your spouse happy.

Don't be like most spouses who get married at the top of their game and then throw on the brakes with that first handful of wedding cake. Don't be like me and get lazy. The mirror will never lie for you. And your spouse will not lose all of their sensory functions at one time. So, you are going to have to do better than I did and wake up to the fact that attractiveness doesn't just happen. Youthful metabolism will crap out and gravity will always win. But you can fight the good fight against their terrorism and do your best.

Why?

Because your spouse wants you to look nice. They are not happy about being married to an unattractive person who has become that way due to delusion and laziness. They are not going to be turned on by the fact that you are a little better looking than Big Bob up the street or more stylish than Color-blind Carla at the Cupcake Shoppe.

Author's Rant: I know that we live in a moronic beauty-obsessed culture that makes you feel bad for not looking like a celebrity. I am not suggesting Botox or plastic surgery here. I am just saying to do all you can to maximize the outer beauty you have left. It is not that difficult to drop a few pounds, have the upper-lip waxed, use Pro-Activ, shave the neck hair, and get an outfit or two put together. Rembrandt toothpaste might even be in order. You do not have to be a cover model - just don't jam donuts in daily or wear 6-year old tighty-whities and expect your partner to be impressed.

*One final issue to address: Do not enter into the silent and deadly pact with your spouse to *let yourselves go* together. This is a common agreement made at the Unity Candle. "I will gorge myself on Little Debbies and you may drink as much beer as you like, my dear! And not only will we both literally grow together, but we will get diabetes and experience lethargy together."

That's not love and it's not lovely. It just makes the "Until Death do us Part" vow that much more imminent.

**I am not trying to rip on anyone who has some physical issue that cannot be helped. If you don't fit anywhere onto this beauty culture continuum due to some uncontrollable defect, keep your head held high, live this life well because it is just a breath anyway, and feel free to make rude, sarcastic comments to "good-looking people" about how bad they make you feel.

***And for all the rest of us who are beauty challenged, remember that physical beauty definitely fades over time. Andre Agassi went bald, Nicole Kidman will have dark eye circles, and Princess Kate will most likely grow unsightly ear hair.

Okay, Fellow Winners who became Owners who became Losers who are now seeking to become Winners once again: Let's pick up the pace a bit and race forward into some more Best Practices and become better together.

Best Practice #3:

Beware the Major Marriage Killers

This is not your typical "marriage killer" section. I'm not going to talk about having better communication, recognizing body language, arguing correctly or the regular stuff about "not going to bed angry" and making sure to have regular bouts of sex so that cheating does not happen. Nope. I live in the real freaking world with you. Who needs repetition of the basics?

This section is instead going to challenge you to take a look at how the different parts of a *regular* life in our *irregular* culture can weaken marriage to the point of death. In other words, the following will show you how normal things are more responsible for divorces than the abnormal.

Anatomy of a Marriage Murder Part A.

Our Standard of Living (S.O.L): Becoming the Joneses

Most Americans believe there is a base financial "Standard of Living." In other words, if you were to ask a majority of people living in the United States to show you their budgetary necessities, the realistic ones will report the following line items:

o Smart Phone with a Good Data plan (iPhone with five pages of apps).

o Decent housing in a secure part of town (rent or mortgage payment for enough safe space to sleep and store food).

o Health Insurance (Don't get into an ambulance without it!!!)

o Car (monthly payments if you want to drive something acceptable among your colleagues.)

o Car Insurance (for when you are texting and accidentally sideswipe my car or that guy on the bicycle.)

o Basic Car Maintenance (oil, air filters, air conditioners, engine blocks)

o Gasoline (The SUV only gets 5 MPG, baby.)

o Debt Payments (school loans or 10 credit card minimum payments) o Cable or Dish Television with TiVo (Throw in some Netflix and a sports package.)

o High Speed Internet on reasonably new Computer (Apple preferred with fastest OS or a non-infected PC – yeah right…)

o Utilities (Electricity, Trash, Water, SUV's, etc.)

o Entertainment/Fun Money (without more diversion, I might die of boredom.)

o Books and Magazines (US Mag, Sports Illustrated, and some *Fight Club* will make your mind pop with pop culture philosophies.)

o Starbucks (I had to add this as a separate line item because coffee is our main drug of choice. And it isn't cheap.)

o Gifts (Christmas, Valentine's, anniversaries, birthdays, Mother's Day, Father's Day, etc.)

o Restaurant Money ("Hamburger Helper be damned. Tonight we dine out!")

o Groceries ("I have only half a pantry of food at home. I'd better fill up a basket or two and grab a few four-packs of hip, effervescent, live-culture Kombucha.")

o Hygiene Products (Best to invest heavy here. From hair to mouth to feet.)

o Laundromat/Dry Cleaning Money (quarters, detergent, etc.)

o Vacation Savings (One must escape from their everyday, right?)

o Clothing (new fedoras and skinny ties for all the hipsters out there.)

o Furniture and Décor Money (from cool couches to knick-knacks to "must-have" yard statues.)

o Life Insurance Premiums (I like to gamble on my death happening soon, so I get term-life.)

o Savings (Somebody once told me having a little extra cash stashed away might be a smart move just in case the country enters a financial and/or political crisis.)

o Vices (We all do messed up stuff so we might as well admit it and put money aside for our impulsivities.)

o Childcare (If you have little versions of yourself, they cost about double what you are worth.)

o Pet Care (dogs, cats, snakes, fish, birds and/or turtles need to be fed and housed appropriately)

o General Giving (charity, tithe, generosity and/or for the dude on the corner with the sign who needs some bus ticket money.)

Now since this is a budget for the majority, it does not necessarily reflect those who are living intentionally simple lives or reflect those living extravagant lives. The above simply reflects the line items you are going to find on most budget lists in the American "middle" class.

What do these line items reveal about us?

At the very least, they probably reveal we expect a certain number of things to be in our lives so that our lives can be considered balanced and maybe even good. They probably also reveal either a Standard of Living we have grown accustomed to due to family upbringing, or a Standard of Living being experienced by our current peer group.

This Standard of Living is considered fairly common among those in the middle and even among the lower middle class. *And since it is considered common, it has become a Standard of Living that most people feel they deserve. If someone were to subtract too many of those items, you would find that most individuals would respond with frustration — some of them acting as if you are starving them from the basics of life as they understand it. Many people who have to live without some of these things can stand the setback only temporarily and they do what it takes to get these things back so as not to appear strange among those around them. Or maybe the bigger motivation is so they can live the comfortable and convenient life they have either already had (or have been told they can have in this culture).*

I want to be clear here that these aforementioned items *are not* considered parts of The American Dream. *These are instead considered to be part of the "American Standard Reality" — nothing really to dream about, but rather to expect, upon waking each morning.* (For some, as a result of our spoiled indoctrination and a mindset that says we deserve almost everything that appears on our TV screens and in magazine ads, the absence of too many of them would be decried as *The American Nightmare*.)

I cannot tell you how many times I have seen people hit near emotional and mental breakdowns when their cell phones and/or computers break down. I am part of this same group who panics when the cable goes off or my car does not start or the house won't get warm enough. I carry on like a wild man with his Master's Degree in Complaint until something gets done about what 95% of the world would consider simple loss of *extravagant luxury*.

What is your Standard of Living?

What are the line items within it?

How do you react when you lose or have to subtract from these line items?

How would you feel if you had to remove several of them from your life?

Those are important questions to consider as we tie the Standard of Living into the reality of marriages. What does the Standard of Living have to do with Marriage Killing? What potential problems does this Standard of Living cause?

Within a marriage, a problem pops up when there is a significant difference in Standard of Living from one spouse to the other. If one partner has a lot more "necessary" line items on their Standard list than their spouse or if one of them simply assigns different amounts (higher or lower) to an agreed upon list, there will be an immediate struggle. This reveals a difference in expectation, and if it is significant enough, one partner can feel ripped off by the "less than" they are living under; or the other will feel the extra pressure it takes to provide the money to make the higher expectation happen for their spouse.

For instance, if the husband believes a membership at a golf course is a necessary line item so that he can "socialize with business colleagues" (read: "drink with buddies") and let off some steam by smacking a white ball towards a flag (snap-hooking it into the weeds and then kicking it into the fairway) but is told by his frugal and hardworking wife this is too expensive and suggests that he try mini-golfing with Yellow Page coupons once a week instead, there will be much gnashing of teeth.

Another example is if one of the partners grew up very wealthy and got used to having a personal chef, masseuse, and nanny as "normal," while the other partner grew up on Chef Boyardee, neck cramps, and insane Aunt Kathleen as their caretaker; there is going to be some major push and pull when their budget gets rolled out.

Another potential problem arises regardless of the difference of Standards and it accompanies the answer to the following question: How are couples going to attain whatever agreed upon Standard of Living they have set?

Outside of bank robbing husbands and wives, most of us choose to do the "normal" thing to get what we "need," which is WORK.

Anatomy of a Marriage Murder Part B.

OVERWORKing is Living?

To make sure a Standard of Living is reached (average $3500 - $4300 monthly without children), most couples have to work. And work not only takes up a lot of time, but it also tends to leave the worker exhausted, frustrated, and disappointed by the end of an eight to ten-hour day. One important thing to consider here is that because we typically begin the day with work, it tends to get the best of us.

Let's explore some reality of how work affects marriages.

In the morning upon waking, most couples are in their own form of mad rush to get ready for the day. They make some small talk, ask simple questions, but their full selves are not into the marriage because they are usually thinking about the workday ahead. (Because work is a worshipped part of our culture, we allow it to be a consuming concern within our thoughts during almost every waking moment.) Our minds are filled with inboxes and projects and possible promotions and the rest of our employment lusts. We typically have our heads committed to the vocational ladder we need to climb that day. And why not? For the love of security, acceptance, reputation, and perception, we work and work just like we've been taught since school began. Most of us have allowed overwork to become an absolute "have-to."

Work Ethic is something almost everyone agrees is an ideal worth serving.

As a result, the typical married couple forges through the morning ritual, says their requisite "I love you(s)," exchanges hugs and kisses and then they go off in their separate vehicles to their separate buildings to work alongside men and women of similar trainings. And it is here that most of each person's fuel is used up.

Trying to live up to job description expectations just as they lived up to 18-20 years of GPA pressures, husbands and wives go about giving all they have intellectually, emotionally, and relationally at their job site not only to gain approval, but also to maintain their position, which can give them what they need to sustain the "Standard of Living" detailed earlier.

I want to reiterate a piece of the above paragraph again as a point of emphasis: Individuals go to work and are expected to make use of their whole selves.

Most of us at an employment site/office have to deal with other people. And in our dealings, we are expected to have all sorts of conversations, remember things about other people's lives, be a friendly, good teammate alongside colleagues who have all sorts of personality types, flaws, pasts, idiosyncrasies, moralities and opinions. These relational expectations can be very draining. *We might have chosen our spouses, but we rarely get to choose those we work with. This means we give up extra emotional, relational, and intellectual energy simply to keep everyone around us impressed enough to ensure a good evaluation.*

And then, since there is typically an ominous competitive spirit beckoning us to move upward within the workplace, we often have to watch our backs while trying to gain notice from senior leadership by constantly living up to our résumés. None of us wants to be left behind. We want to be seen as worthy of promotion and as someone valuable enough to deserve a raise and/or a recognition/award. Those sorts of movements, which usually stroke our egos and lead us closer to our dreams of self-actualization, mean more responsibility and often more hours at the job (minimum jump from 40 to 50 hours per week).

Since this "career climber" mentality lines up with our embedded American Worldview and gives us a very real rush from the mix of busyness, victory, and achievement, many of us make the trade and assume that our spouse will be happy because we are contributing to the bottom line of provision.

The shared belief might be: As long as we move up, we can make more money and can both keep buying more cool stuff with greater speed and impulsivity. With more money, we can find ways into better neighborhoods and nicer school systems, so that we can experience an abundant, secure, luxurious lifestyle supposedly promised to everyone with First-World blood.

To ensure that this upward movement continues, the customers/clients we serve must get our full attention and their problems must be solved. We must listen to them and help them. We must also be incredibly attentive to our bosses who tell us how we can best bring value to the organization. Even if our bosses are boring morons who inherited the place we work in, we have to show them respect and make sure they are treated well, which takes effort - especially if ass-kissing is somewhat necessary to remain in the CEO's good graces.

Finally, there is the actual work to be done. Regardless of the job, be it in an office, massage school, or gas station, there are projects to be initiated, processes to be followed, policies to maintain, and mostly a set of the most mundane tasks on the planet that are yours to handle.

While it might be hard to believe, some people really like their jobs. But no job is without its inherent frustrations. And hardly anyone comes away from their eight to twelve hours a day feeling refreshed and more energized than when they began (unless they work as a sleep study subject or mattress tester). In fact, most humans, whether they love or loathe their vocations, often leave them behind feeling undone and stressed. Those who are in jobs that do not match their passions (the dead-end "what am I doing here filling out paperwork all day" jobs), will not only be wiped out, but also most likely angry, disappointed, and longing for something to change as they watch their lives slip away into an existentialist pit of dream-death.

Now, here is the point of bringing up all the above: The marriage partners who are returning home from this sort of long day hanging out among relative strangers, are not the same humans who left home that morning. They are coming back to their spouse (or both are coming back to their spouses) with less energy, less calm, less patience, less desire to serve, and really less "good-spouseyness" as a whole. There has been depletion on the daily scale and probably some longer-term and irreversible erosion on the deeper levels of the partner or partners. An important word here for what happens is Subtraction.

Work subtracts from us valuable relational pieces and just pays us with GREEN PAPER for the life takeaway.

But is it worth it?

When you consider the potential costs of this subtraction on a marriage, is it really worth it?

Two people working for so many reasons (some noble, some not) and for most of their waking hours finally reach their home bases after long, tiresome days and come together with much less to give out to their partners than what their partners want, need, and expect.

Can you now see how Standard of Living and Work contribute to weaker relationships at home?

Let's be honest, when we give out so much at one place, we hope our post-work life will be a place of Addition.

Most spouses hope their partners will be there for them as a giver, an addition, a servant and a friend. Someone who will listen to them, care about them, comfort them and remind them who they are. Someone who will allow them to unwind, eat without manners, debrief, drop off their résumés at the door, and remove the masks so they can just be loved for a while.

We do not want to get home and face another set of tasks. We do not want to work hard again to get the chores done or take care of the finances. We do not want to be bothered by a home-boss. We don't want the person we love to project their day of frustrations onto us because they can finally let it spew outside of the "have-to" culture of work. We often just want to kick back, rest, take on a fun diversion, or go numb with TV set characters who ask nothing of us but to watch them live out worse disasters than we have or see them achieve the things we cannot.

In most cases, the return home during the workweek is a drop down zombie-land of survival saturated by caffeine fixes, mad scrambles to get kids' homework done, followed by getting them to bed (using Jedi negotiation techniques) and then, finally, some small talk among lovers who share space on soft couches catching up on TiVo.

Anatomy of a Marriage Murder Part C.

Shared Subtraction

One problem with this described reality is that both partners within the marriage typically feel the same way when they get home (either from a career role or from a day of kids and/or innumerable errands). Wherever they came home from, *both partners want and both partners need.* This usually means each partner is looking to the other partner to be their Addition, but neither of them have much to add to anyone or anything. And if that expectation exists for each individual to be what the other wants and needs, there can be a lot of hurt and disappointment (even resentment) when it is not pulled off by either. There is a lingering sense of letdown and this letdown can erode a marriage.

Simple Summary: Upon arrival at home, our lovers are not loving us the way we want and need. We are not loving them the way they want and need. And quiet questions may begin to rise up in our minds: *So why did we marry in the first place? Was it so we could share space with a fellow subtraction robot of a husband or wife?*

Anatomy of a Marriage Murder Part D.

Home-work

Another problem to place next to the one above is that *there is work* to be done at the home-base and both partners need to share the assignments and duties. Despite a shared exhaustion and common stress, home, like work, has its "have-to dos."

Bills have to get paid, budgets have to get a closer look, mail has to be sifted through and handled appropriately, food has to be conjured up, the yard has to get mowed, furniture has to be dusted, windows and mirrors need some Windexing, the bathtub and toilet require a decent scrubbing, the trash has to be gathered and taken to better places, dishes have to be washed, clothes have to be loaded, soaped, dried, folded and hung, sheets have to be changed, home calls have to be returned, the carpet needs vacuuming, the car(s) need(s) to be filled with gas, the dog needs a walk and probably a bath, etc. (And if/when you have children, add about one trillion other duties to this list.)

Home-work is a reality. And besides the personal subtraction these duties can create for individuals, there are other potential issues here. For instance, if one partner is more dedicated to home-work than the other, this can cause all sorts of problems. Also problematic is if one partner's idea of completing the home-work means doing it at an A+ level and the other is content with a D+.

Both of these common situations can lead to one partner becoming an angry taskmaster and sort of the boss over the home while the other becomes the lazy spouse who "never helps" but who is pissed off that they are being labeled, griped out, and most of all, pushed to do more when they might be running on empty.

(Truth is, this might not even be an issue of dedication versus laziness. It might be that one partner has just prioritized home-work as a top emphasis upon leaving their *paid* work while the other partner has prioritized some rest and rejuvenation before launching into automaton duties. Neither priority is necessarily right or wrong, but it should be discussed so that an understanding of a good order is agreed upon.)

Anatomy of a Marriage Murder Part E.

Over-Availability

Another problem, which is becoming more and more of an issue in marriage is what I call increased availability. With smart phones, laptops, and various tablets dominating the market and dominating our attentions with their daily expansions of "distractions on the go," we tend to lose track of our spouses, even when they are present. We take cell calls in the middle of date nights, read and send texts during foreplay, check voicemails with one ear and barely hear our spouse with the other ear, download apps and play on them instead of figuring out some sort of fun we can engage in with our partner, answer emails and surf an endless web world instead of probing deeper into the life of the one non-Skyped person in the day. We basically become the most networked and yet most isolated human beings because we satisfy cravings by adding the new and exciting, which is now delivered to our instantly gratified fingertips on portable machines that fill something our tired spouses are too tired to fill.

We never make ourselves *unavailable* to our jobs or our technologies because we don't want to have to face the odd silence of our marriage, which might be disappointing and frustrating in comparison.

Is this true for you?

When you get home, how available are you to your technologies?

How focused are you on your spouse?

Be honest…

Adding up everything above, what might a marriage "equal?"

$$A + B + C + D + E = \underline{\hspace{4cm}}$$

= Tired conversations often filled with nothing new (debriefing the past eight to ten hours and sharing about colleagues/clients whom our partners barely know)

= Distracted time together (with some sort of machine getting in the way of intimacy)

= Projected anger and frustrations (taking out the stress of the day on the other)

= Arguments about respect, bills, priorities, parenting the kids, present and future decisions, tiny and ridiculous miscellaneous things

= Proclaimed disappointments about how expectations are not being met

= Misunderstandings and miscommunications

= Shared viewing of your passions and hopes being traded in for what reality demands

= Spiritual dryness and lack of desire (due to lack of time)

= Complaints about feeling stuck/trapped coupled with a proclaimed inability to escape

= Good sex substituted for three-minute quickies

= Throwing yourselves into the lives of the children

= Blaming and faultfinding

= Questioning original decision to marry the one you have and growing discontent with the person who doesn't meet your needs

= Unsuccessful attempts to re-shape each other into someone who meets our wants/needs (attempting to change our spouse into a better fit for our comfort)

= Desires/Fantasies about some *one* or some *thing* new and "healthy" to add ripples to a seemingly stagnant, banal and empty life (babies, new job, new possessions, new community, new hobbies, etc.)

= Desires/Fantasies about some *one* or some *thing* new and "unhealthy" to add ripples to a seemingly stagnant, banal, and empty life (mistress/mister, excess alcohol or other life numbing substances, "Eat, pray, love" syndrome, etc.)

= Just stick it out as tired and frustrated people while hoping for some miracle "lottery ticket change"

= Settle for the way things are in a fatalistic manner rather than seeking positive changes

= Obey Oprah and get happy no matter what it takes

= Start your own double/secretive life to get what you want/need from someone or something else (See Don Draper on *Mad Men*)

**Emotional and physical affairs are usually with someone with whom you spend a lot of work time or distraction time (those who ask nothing of you but want to be your giver and those who have the energy and time to be your love language translator)

= Get expensive marriage counseling with someone who may or may not know how to address your deeper issues

= Short-term separation during which living arrangements are divided up to take pressure off of each party and a more romantic relationship is rebuilt

= Divorce (Horror-Show explosion of bitterness and anger or a possible civil event where both agree that it was just harder than they thought it would be)

= Date and then try again with someone else who is going to be both just as good and just as bad as the one you stepped away from

****

How have things added up for you?

Can you find your relationship somewhere in the descriptions above?

Is the regular, normal life equation described above leading you to lose some of the best parts of your marriage?

What can we do to stop this particular cycle from happening?

Some Suggestions for Stopping the Marriage Killers before they can successfully add you to their Victim List:

(Not all of the below will be possible for every reader, but most of it is possible with some good planning. Do your best and hopefully you will not have to face what far too many struggle with.)

o Be a person with a fantastic work ethic and an excellent attitude. Work hard and be a good person while you are working.

o Stop being so busy with what the world tells you is important. While the world may insist something is a "have to do," most things are not crucial at all.

o Get busy with your spouse. Take that however you like. Relational things are not optional.

o Work fewer hours per week if you can.

o Train for a career that allows you to work from home/work virtually.

o Determine your Standard of Living budget based on how much you will be making at your job(s). Don't set your S.O.L. and then work as much as it will take to reach it.

o Move to a city or a country with a lower cost of living.

o Quit thinking that you deserve what you desire. You are not entitled to the newest, coolest, or best just because commercials tell you so.

o Find contentment outside of materialism and money. Stop buying more and more stuff.

- Stop basing your worth on your achievements and advancements.

- Learn to love quiet boredom. Ripples of excitement are overrated.

- Be technologically unavailable at least four hours every waking day.

- Trade information with your spouse about "the ideal scenario" for when you get home after work.

- Lower your over-the-top expectations for everyone and everything. Joyfully accept the "real."

- Don't seek instant gratification in any sphere.

- Don't live as if greed is good.

- Avoid the *Spend Now and Pay Later* cycle of debt. Credit card usage is not part of the normal life.

- Quit worrying about what others are thinking of you or what they will think about you.

- Focus on what you do have and give thanks as much as you can for it.

- If you have children, enjoy the little moments where you actually connect. Definitely do not pressure them because of your own frustrations/disappointments.

- Don't let machines make you happy.

- Don't worry about living up to your potential.

- Determine marriage is forever even when romance is not.

- Don't do whatever it takes to be selfishly happy (add, subtract, change.)

- Compromise on the home-work and its timing.

Best Practice #4:

Handling Change Well _When_ It Happens

When we get married, we are usually marrying someone whom we have known for a limited amount of time, which means we have seen them respond and react to _some_ circumstances and conditions, but not to every possible situation. We know them, but we don't know "the future them."

In light of that, here are some important questions: What happens when our "spouse of the present" gets hit by a major storm in the future and they become someone we do not recognize anymore? How do we respond if/when their attitudes and behaviors shift in significant and permanent ways? Can we handle the poorer, the sicker, and the _worse-r_ sides of our lover when those changes are not seasonal waves but marital tsunamis?

It is quite easy to fall in love when conditions are good, and simpler to say, "I do" when circumstances lean toward the better and richer and healthier sides of the vows we make. Marriages that begin in those places are sweet. But, marriages usually do not stay in those places because life is what it is. Sometimes it is sunny and sometimes it is not. And as couples we have to learn to roll well together with the fun of the _shiny_ as well as with the pain of the storms.

This is easier said than done.

When we commit to our marriages, most of us have had enough life experience to realize the realities of the human condition – how it gives and takes – how it includes joy and depression – justice and unfairness. But it is rare for an individual or a couple to prepare themselves for the level-ten life storms, which can transform the bad into the horrific for long periods of time.

Consider some examples and how you might respond if the following happened to you or to your spouse:

o   Sicknesses/Diseases creating extreme pain and requiring maxed out credit cards to try to beat it.

o   Unexpected physical tragedies leaving a spouse burned, immobilized, disabled, and/or unable to communicate.

o   Loss of a child.

o   Long-term unemployment with growing debt, frustration, and the repossession of one's identity and confidence (as well as a home and car).

o   Betrayal by a close friend.

o   The death of a dream. Recognition that what you thought you were made for is never going to happen and now one or both of you have to settle for the "regular" clock in and clock out existence.

o   A string of "Almosts" which come up, raise your hopes and then demolishes them all like bowling pins (constant disappointment). As Solomon once said: "Hopes deferred make the heart sick." And to have one or two heartsick spouses underneath one roof is too much to bear for long.

o   Mid-life crisis/Nervous Breakdowns/Struggles with Aging.

There are a lot more I could mention, but the point is not to specify the storm as much as it is to speak about the aftermath of such storms.

What do these storms do to people?

How do these storms change people?

And what happens to a marriage with stockpiled wreckage coming between two people who have been altered by the wind and the waves of such storms?

What happens when a storm rocks and negatively transforms just one of the persons in a marriage and the other is left to try and respond correctly even though they have no idea how to respond?

So many tough questions.

Here is an important truth:

We marry one person but we *will* end up with a different one. Can you handle that? Will you allow for love to flex and adapt to a new version of your spouse, even if they are sicker, poorer, and worse?

Will you allow for love to flex for your spouse if the *better* and *wealthier* happen to transform them into someone different?

What if your spouse ends up drastically different?

What if she takes a sharp left onto a dirt road at menopause and/or he hits mid-life crisis time and seems to become the oddest stranger you've ever met?

Time and chance happen to everyone. Good and bad change affects everyone. And sometimes life gets so hard that couples don't know what to do to sustain their covenants to one another. Thinking through the tough realities of life and understanding how they can beat down a perfectly good marriage is important for everyone who marries. To have discussed a plan of survival and to have made firm determinations about a collective response will help form a kind of future shelter for the times of shock when neither partner is able to think clearly or decide well. You'll be better off and have a better chance of making it though a storm if you are "storm prepared."

Best Practice #5:

Know how to make decisions together

Do you have a shared decision-making framework, which works for both you and your significant other?

A brilliant (but anonymous) human once said, "Life is made up of decisions stacked upon decisions. As we decide, so we live. To live well, one must decide well and do so consistently in every category of life."

When I look at my life in light of those sentences, I can see how both large and small decisions have led me to where I am vocationally, emotionally, educationally, spiritually, and relationally. I am a product of my decisions. Surely there have been strong people and powerful circumstances, which have influenced me and prompted me to choose one course over another, but ultimately I have been allowed the choice to go this way or that. I have been given the freedom to sow with my choices and then to harvest the consequences. No one else is really to blame for what I bring out of the soil of my life.

These realizations have led me to believe I need to take my decisions more seriously. I do not want to make decisions haphazardly or choose based on my feelings/impulses, because those decisions typically suck. So, I have chosen to create a decision-making framework, which acts as a filter to help me make wise decisions on a more consistent basis so that my life looks more like I want it to look.

In the relational setting, especially within marriage, having an agreed upon/shared decision-making framework is huge. Since you two are in this life together as a unified "one," you do not want either partner dominating the decision-making process. Just because I have created a decision-making framework, which I think is smart, it does not mean my significant other will or should bend to its directives.

For as you make decisions, so you live and so will you become. Apply that to a marriage and the truth becomes: As you make wise decisions together, so will your marriage form into something where mutual happiness can occur.

Seriously, marriage happiness is often demolished when the power of decision-making is claimed by one person or is claimed together but in a random fashion.

So, what is your decision-making framework at this stage of life? Are you happy with the life you have or have your "stacked decisions" led you to a place of deep discontent?

If you are married or engaged to someone, do you have an agreed upon decision-making framework, which will help lead you as "one" toward the best plans and purposes for your life and the lives of those you affect?

See below for an exercise that might help you form your own most effective decision-making process.

Exercise: Assessing a mutual decision-making framework

An actual decision-making framework for couples has been written below and it has some good stuff in it. Steal, add, and subtract as much as you like and then form a standard framework that best works for you.

A Shared Decision-Making Example:

o   Do not trust in "distance experts" who purport to know what is best for you. Read their self-help data, but know that most "experts" are asked to comment in ways that sway a *general populace* rather than provide answers for your specific situation.

o   Do not decide based solely on advice given by those who love you. Take their counsel but do not immediately act upon it, because often those who love you: A. Want what they *think* is best for you and/or B. Want what is best for them.

o   Do not decide based on what your peers or colleagues are doing. Conformity is a major influencer. Feel free to "fit out" rather than to "fit in."

o   Do not be influenced by media. Regardless of what Huffington, Ellen, or Elle magazine suggest, go with what you know to be true at a deeper level. Newspapers, newscasts, and magazines spin you in different directions for their purposes.

o   Ignore commercials. Every Kiss does not begin with Kay, diamonds are not forever, and owning a Mercedes is not going to drive you to a life without regret.

o Do not do what you have always done. Each moment is new and requires new considerations.

o Don't avoid what you have never done. Fear of the unknown keeps us cautiously choosing similar roads and possibly not choosing the best roads.

o Beware of your Desires, because they can be big liars. The "Want" inside of us is not necessarily bad, but it can lead us to lie, cheat, and steal to get some golden carrot. Thus, always check your desires and motives.

o Feelings are also deceptive and cannot be trusted to guide you. Marriages that run on feeling are going to be short-term and potentially cruel.

o Do not believe every reputable religious person who tells you that you should go in a certain direction, even if they claim to have heard from God. See the biblical story in I Kings 13 and realize that everyone lies and that every word from even the most spiritual person requires a *check-in* with everything else in this framework.

o Same thing goes for reputable therapists, psychologists, and psychiatrists. Just because they studied a lot of books and put in thousands of hours working with *real people* does not mean they can grasp the nuances of your individual and shared histories enough to advise you correctly on specific decisions. Appreciate them as generalists who skillfully listen for patterns and can suggest several options.

o Do not make decisions to avoid judgment from others (perception-based decisions). Sometimes your decisions are going to offend others or make them think you are an idiot. Accept that and move forward.

o Do not make decisions to please others. People-pleasing will lead you onto crooked roads marked by U-turns and dead fads.

o Do not be rushed into a decision. Just because the used car dealer, realtor or the telemarketer tells you "it is the last one" or that the deal they have offered is only on the table for today, let it go until you have given it adequate thought and have counted the cost.

o The Road Less Traveled might be less traveled because there is a killer about a mile down the way. Do not necessarily go with the different just because it is different.

o Do not judge the "consequences" of your decision too quickly. Just because it starts rough does not mean you need to turn around yet. On the same token, just because it begins like a calm lazy river, does not mean you are heading to a safe splashdown.

o Don't be prideful about your decisions and think you are always right. As a powerful man once said, "There is a way that seems right to a person, but in the end it leads to death."

o Think about how your decision might positively and negatively affect those close to you in the present and future. Consider how "unintended consequences" might come into play.

o Make sure both parties/both spouses being equally affected by the decision are given equal say in the decision process. Do not be the singular bully and force things to go your way every time. Do not be passive aggressive in your manipulation either. Seek true consensus on major issues out of respect for one another.

o Avoid the extremes of impulsivity, compulsivity, and indecision. The first two are too quick and the latter equals immobility. Combine solid wisdom with a pacing that is acceptable for both of you.

o If a decision ends up being the wrong one, do not redact history to make yourself into the "victim who knew it was a bad idea." Being that sort of jerk-historian who always blames their significant other for past *consensus decisions gone wrong* is deserving of a reprimand.

o If a decision ends up being the wrong one and you used someone else's advice/guidance to motivate you to go that "wrong way," do not be angry or frustrated at them. At the end of the day, you allowed yourself to be influenced by a frail, fallible human and then you used your own free will to decide. The buck stops with you, unless there was a gun held to your head. Then you might have a good argument.

o If you believe in prayer and pray about which way to go and feel some strong urging to go one way over the other and it ends up making your lives harder, don't get bitter. Too many people are mad at God for supposedly messing up their worlds.

o Don't let your "consensus mistakes" drive you into a life-minefield. Many couples make a wrong move on a mid-level to high-level decision early in their marriage and then refuse to take steps in any direction for fear of having their shared life blown to bits. Risk freely and take your shots. You will choose the wrong things a lot, even if it was thought out, felt right, was priced right, smelled right, and Wikipedia assured you it was going to be right.

o Stay within the parameters of the American social contract in most cases and stop at most red lights. But if life calls for a minor or major rebellion that takes you outside of the social contract's boundaries, do not let "good" or "bad" legal limits keep you from being counter-cultural. Sometimes you have to cross into the room marked, "No Entry" to find what you both have been seeking. Be smart but brave.

o Avoid use of the phrase, "I told you so" - Especially when it is too late to fix a bad decision.

o Do not make "secret decisions." Secret decisions are usually made by a person because they know their significant other would not approve of their decision. Secret decisions have consequences that are typically not so easy to keep secret. Secret decisions are often driven by unchecked desires and/or uncontrollable addictions. Secret decisions are kept secret using deception and evasion and can grow into a secret life. Secret lives are destructive to most marriages, e.g., "Breaking Bad" TV show for an example.

o Don't spend too much time regretting a bad decision. Sure, some consequences deserve a little mourning and even possibly some deep thought, but don't sit around wishing you had not gone a certain direction for too long. Regret typically helps nothing. Recover from a bad decision by making some good decisions.

o After making some decisions, review the good and bad consequences to see if there are any lessons, which can be learned from them.

o Consensus is not always a necessity as marriage goes on (especially for the minor and insignificant). In fact, sometimes it is overkill. But practicing it early on and making it a standard habit is good for both partners. Still in the areas where one partner knows more, has more experience with and/or is much more interested in a specific life choice, that person should be given more weight in the decision-making process. For instance, if a husband knows a ton more about computers than his wife does and the household has decided to purchase one, let the dude buy the Apple and move on. (No need to fight about Alt-Ctrl-Del and Spyware for years.)

What do you think about this decision-making framework? What parts of it make sense to you? What would you include/leave out? Why?

There is certainly more to say about good decision-making, but I will leave you to add and subtract for yourselves. Just make sure to take the creation of this framework very seriously from the very beginning so that your marriage is not one of stacked-up discontent, misplaced blame, and total regret. Filter your relational, educational, locational, vocational, financial, material, and spiritual decisions through a well-formed framework. Your life will be consistently interesting.

Do you have a decision-making process that helps you filter out desires, past experiences and strong influences?

If you have been married a while, how have you shared decision-making? Has it gone well? What has gone wrong?

Is there an imbalance of power in the decisions made in your marriage?

What lessons can you learn from decisions you have made to do or not do certain things?

Best Practice #6:

Working Together for Transformation

Have you ever taken inventory of what "exists" in your own life? Have you ever taken inventory of what "exists" within your marriage? More important, have you ever thought of marriage as a way to come together as a unified force to transform the world around you into a better place?

Every individual has been given abilities, talents, relationships, connections, affinities, occupations, possessions, gifts, personalities, and training/educated skill sets.

In other words, all of us have an inventory of "goods," which can and which could be aimed at bettering the lives of people around us. In my world, I like to think of it as having a "Life-Box" filled up with various items in it for the sake of adding more light, more kindness, more love, more generosity, and more help to a world that could use more of all of the above.

Once a year, I actually draw a big square on a piece of paper and write out the specifics of my inventory inside and then begin to consider how the individual items and even combinations of things within my Life-Box can be used to make some positive difference in the world around me.

This "Life-Box" keeps me focused on what I have rather than on what I don't have. It makes me thankful and keeps me from complaining. It makes me realize how much I can do to bring value to my sphere of influence.

What might this sort of thinking do when brought into the arena of marriage?

What could happen after marriage when your inventory merges with someone else's inventory?

From my years of counseling others, I have noticed that a significant shift occurs when couples decide to turn themselves into "teams" dedicated to others' goodwill. This can be such a great move for married people. I've watched some very troubled husbands and wives change their perspectives, set aside their life-sucking, problem-generating marital vacuum, focus on a world larger than the one they have been coming home to, put their combined energies behind a social, religious, or even international cause and ultimately bring exciting change to something/someone while bonding in a way that can make their marriage a million times better.

A marriage, if viewed unselfishly, is a multiplication of inventories so transformation can flow from a relationship. I believe more married people need to see how their linked boxes can make them more effective in impacting their shared world. Too few couples see their marriage as a possibility for increased impact. Too few couples realize that working side by side for a larger cause can be a very real solution to erasing their little intra-marriage causes.

**There's really no better prescription to cure the pandemic of selfish, whiny, complaint-filled, entitlement-based marriages than taking this idea seriously by doing what is suggested below.

You ready?

Cool. Then get to work on the next page…

Do the following Exercise: Fill out a Life-Box

Consider the areas below and with your spouse fill in the empty box on the following page with as many specifics as you can. The answers to the following questions will become the contents of your Life-Box.

*What relationships do I have with influential people who are able to move and shake situations in ways that could create significant change? Which people am I friends with who would do anything for me or for a cause I am pushing? What connections do I have that I could share with those who do not have connections?

*What materials or possessions do I have that could be used to make a difference in people's lives? What do I barely use that I could give away?

*What is my life story and how might it be used to inspire others to do significant things? What experiences do I have that might help others progress?

*What natural abilities or skills do I have that could help the world be a better place? What do people tell me I have a lot of potential with? What are people always asking me for help with?

*What have I learned from my years of education in my family and in school that I could pass on to others or use to solve problems outside of myself?

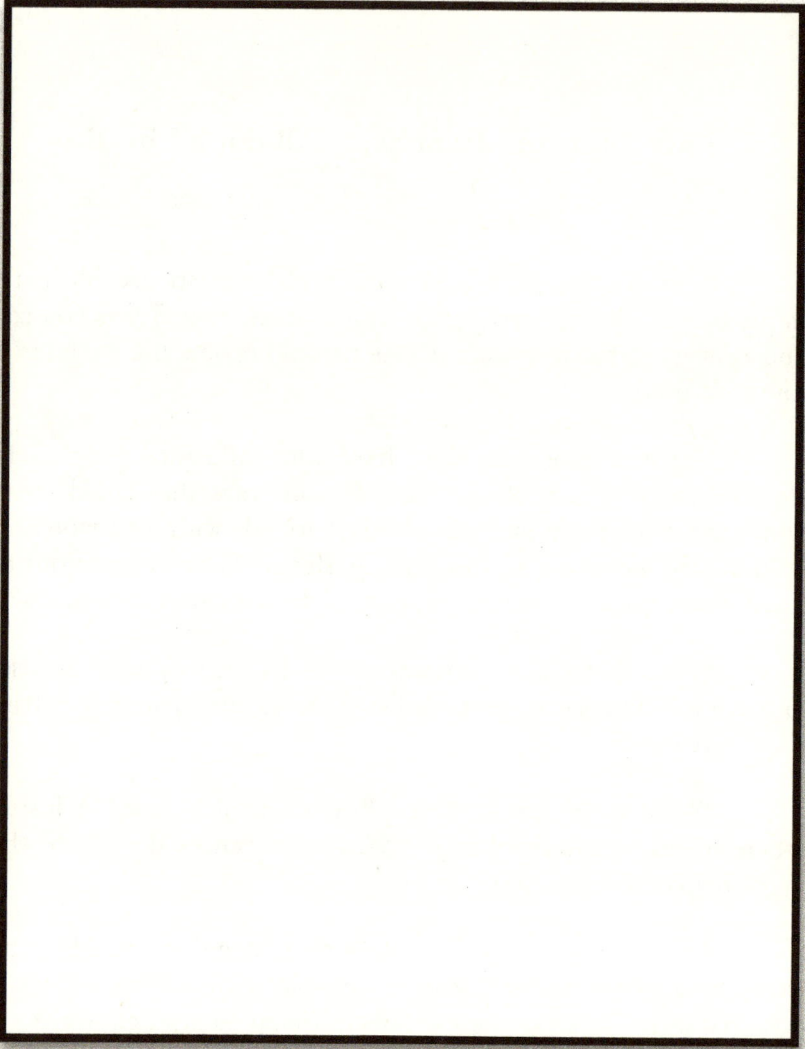

Our Life-Box

Questions to discuss with your spouse

--How can we use what is inside our Life-Boxes:

o   To show love?

o   To do good?

o   To bring justice?

o   To show mercy?

o   To solve problems?

o   To give hope?

o   What do our boxes tell us about gratefulness?

o   What are some important things to bring into our boxes?

o   Are our boxes being used for unselfish acts?

o   Who out there needs what we have to offer?

o   What is one project we can do together this year that will use our Life-Boxes to significantly affect our local community?

o   What is one project we can do together this year that will use our Life-Boxes to significantly affect our world?

To close: When you re-make your relationship into a transformative one and turn your collective eyes toward the brokenness around you, marriage can actually become a powerful source for good in this world.

Best Practice #7:

Humbly Identify Yourselves

How well do you know yourself?

Most people have no clue who they really are. Their identities are typically based on surface descriptions and expectations laid on them by teachers, parents, peers, and culture. Not much personal introspection is done at the deeper emotional levels and thus most people sort of just walk around behaving in a *what you see is what you get* shallowness. The intricacies of their design, the nuances of their internal and external grand beauty, which makes each of them special, all of it, gets shrouded and hidden. They act and react and respond and speak and emote and choose and even marry without much consideration of who they are. They have a name and a driver's license and a social security number and some credit cards allowing them movement in this world of ours, but they lack the sense of self, which must be closely inspected. Without a strong sense of personal identity, those who enter relationships requiring intimacy with a significant other often find themselves ill-equipped to show their deeper selves in vulnerable ways. And when a marriage occurs, depth and vulnerability are expected and pretty much required.

Your spouse will be observing you and wondering why you do what you do and asking why you think the way you think and why you believe the way you believe. Will you have a clue?

You should start asking the questions: Who am I apart from the description everyone else has laid on me all my life? Who is the "deeper me" and how can this *true identity* drive me to act in ways that will support and encourage a human I choose to love for life?

In this section, there are some suggestions you can try that will help you get to know all about you.

Humble Identity:

Become a Personality Guru

Do you know your personality type and have you studied what it means? Are you aware of your significant other's personality so that you can read them in the best possible ways?

There are a lot of personality type tests out there, but I suggest you pay the fifty to one hundred dollars, take a full Myers-Briggs personality test, and have a professional counselor help you understand what the results of that test mean for you as far as your life preferences go. Besides being incredibly accurate in most cases and providing a nice sweeping view of who you are, this test also speaks so much to your relational tendencies. It gives you a solid explanation as to why you do what you do and this explanation can come in very handy during dating, pre-engagement, pre-marital and in-marriage stages of the relational process. As both parties are in discovery mode, sometimes it helps to have this ten-page results document to hand to your possible fiancée so she can know where to offer grace as you do something befitting of your personality.

I know far too many married people who have never taken such a test and I consider this a poor decision. Why not make use of an available tool which effectively points out your natural preferences and tendencies and which can even be a fairly accurate predictor of future actions? There is security to be found within marriages in which both partners can stare into a situation and have

111

a great idea as to how their spouse is going to act within it. Being predictable is not such a bad thing when it comes to most things relational.

Having a really good idea as to how you and your mate will respond to various catalysts and stimuli (because you are aware of your/their personality preferences) gives you a major advantage.

Example 1: If you know that you make most of your decisions rather quickly based on gut feelings because you trust your intuition while your wife prefers to first gather expert advice/as much data as possible before moving in a certain direction, you can stop some huge fights from exploding simply by restraining your seemingly impulsive decisions and giving your wife some time to find out what she needs to "know" so that both of you have input on everything.

Example 2: If you know that your husband is a definite introvert and that he loses energy from being at a large group meeting, you can be more sensitive when you both get home from a party and he behaves negatively according to an emotional tiredness that simply springs from his personality.

Anyway, there are hundreds of ways that personality tests can help you understand one another better so that you can respond and react better and even determine a strategy for détente, or what I call a set of dance moves, that will keep both of you off of one another's toes.

(If you choose to take a test, I suggest you not only get a trained test professional to help you interpret it, but also to invest in the following two books: *Type Talk* by Krueger and Thuesen and *Please Understand Me* by Keirsey and Bates.)

Best Practices Concluded:

Just because an individual, a relationship or an organization employs Best Practices to guide vision, mission, attitude, and everyday movements does not guarantee there will be success in the very long-term. But, on the relational side of things, I have seen plenty of couples use the advice in the previous chapters and achieve some serious turnaround in their collective *marital quality-of-life*.

It is not simple when you are having daily hard times in marriage to gather up the necessary energy to "make a go" at creating something better. But I hope you will start by simply reading this book together with your spouse and discussing how you might prioritize and then apply some of its most relevant points to your current state. You do not have to try to rebuild everything in one day. There are so many macro and micro areas of deep change to go along with my suggested surface level changes that there would be no way you could actually shift *and* also maintain every shift in this book if you only give yourself a short-term timeframe.

This book is not for those of you seeking instant gratification in your marriage. It is for those of you who have committed to forever and are willing to trudge hard toward the most important small transformations throughout life so you will be able to watch your Best Practices turn your relationship into a Best Marriage, where there is tangible joy and daily contentment.

I highly recommend working through this book while at the same time meeting with a qualified therapist who can be a helpful sounding board and well-trained encourager. Even if your marriage is going great at this moment in time, it is smart to build it up with the best practices so that you never have to slide downhill. It's always good to get help before you actually need help.

And for those of you currently struggling couples, I advise you to wipe out any thoughts that your marriage is beyond repair and that you are simply biding time until the right moment arises so you can wave the white flag of surrender. Until both spouses have done all they can, do not give up. Every marriage has seasons of darkness, which can deliver any couple to the brink of divorce. But before you parachute off that cliff and away from the one you once said was your love and life partner, make a firm determination to put the contents of this book into action as you hold onto hope.

I wish you the very best as you take a few steps back from your marriage, get some right perspective, and then work with all your heart and mind to improve your *well-oiled marriage* and/or to renovate a marriage that is dilapidated and nearly condemned. May your marriage be the most beautiful on the block someday as you trust the Best Practices!!!

A Preview of Book Three in the *I Guess I Do: The Ultimate Marriage Survival Guide* series:

- o Understand that the small and seemingly insignificant struggles in your marriage can lead to the end of your entire relationship. (Drowning in the *shallow end* happens a lot.)

- o Over one hundred of the funniest, smartest and most authentic *Thou Shalt Nots* to help you keep your marriage from dying.

- o R.I.P. case studies that will open your eyes to the graveyard possibilities that abound in relationships.

- o Suggestions on how to avoid Marriage Food Poisoning

**All of the above and much more in one of the most creative marriage book series ever conceived by the mind of a seriously dumb husband who is hopefully getting smarter.

About the Author

Ben Donley, author of several books and essays, has many years of experience as a Spiritual and Relational Advisor for those at every stage of the marriage process. Ben is now Head of Acquisitions and the Creative Director for **Jock and Lola Publishing** (Los Angeles and West Texas) and hopes his writing will help some humans both know better *and* do better.

For speaking engagements or retreats, contact Ben at:

Phone: 310-770-2061

http://www.bendonley.com

www.ingramcontent.com/pod-product-compliance
Lightning Source LLC
LaVergne TN
LVHW011335080426
835513LV00006B/366